Climbing

Vernon Coleman

Real-Life Inspirations for the Over 65s

Vernon Coleman is a writer and the author of over 100 other books which have sold over two million hardback and paperback copies in the UK and been translated into 25 languages. Many of his books are available as Kindle books on Amazon. For a list of available eBooks please see Vernon Coleman's author page on Amazon. Vernon Coleman has been growing older for many years and is becoming tolerably good at it.

Dedication

To my wife, my friend, my love, my Antoinette; upon whom I dote and who holds my hand as I wobble and tumble into my dotage.

God gave you beauty and kindness; may He now give you peace, contentment and unlimited delights.

Prologue

These are inspirational true stories to excite the spirit of anyone contemplating old age with fear, suspicion or apprehension.

Introduction

Some of the people in this book achieved great things earlier in life but carried on doing great things long after most people would have retired. But many of the people you will find described below kept their best until later; only achieving greatness when they were well past the official age of retirement. Some did so because they were freed from day to day drudgery; others because they allowed themselves to meet their dreams head on. Some changed course and did something entirely new once they reached their late 60s or beyond.

This isn't a book about people who simply managed to live a long life.

It is a book about people who did amazing, extraordinary, often great things at a time of life when most people are content to look back on what has already happened in their lives, rather than look forward to what may be about to happen. This is a book about people who never let go of life, about people who were never afraid to have adventures, about people who were brave enough to take risks and to accept whatever challenges life threw at them. I have, with one notable exception, ignored Kings, Queens and Popes who achieved great things late in life since their achievements were, to a certain extent, preordained. Within the age groups the individuals mentioned are listed in no particular order.

The human brain doesn't shrink or perish or deteriorate with age. The people on this list are not exceptional in that they retained their faculties, their ambitions and their determination. They are exceptional only in that they continued to make use of their lives and ignored the commonly held suspicion that old age and senility are synonymous.

4

There are, of course, many more inspiring stories than I have included here. For example, Frank Schearer, a retired physician, was still water skiing at the age of 100. The Rolling Stones were still rocking around the world when they were all in their 70s. Being over 70 didn't stop Rod Stewart, Tom Jones, Englebert Humperdinck, Van Morrison, Neil Diamond, Elton John, Shirley Bassey, Cliff Richard or Tina Turner from touring and performing. Clint Eastwood was still directing and starring in movies in his late 80s.

I have chosen to start this list with individuals aged 66 since the age of 65 was arbitrarily chosen as the usual age of retirement in Western countries.

At the age of 66

Sir John Betjeman CBE – born in 1906 in London, England, was a poet, broadcaster and writer of essays about English places and buildings. He became Poet Laureate of England in 1972. He held the post until his death in Cornwall at the age of 77, and is still widely regarded as the most popular poet to have held that position.

Edgar Rice Burroughs – Chicago born but of English ancestry, was the author of nearly 80 novels including the Tarzan books. At the age of 66, he became a war correspondent and was one of the oldest U.S. war correspondents during World War II. Burroughs had been in Honolulu at the time of the Japanese attack on Pearl Harbour.

Herbert Marcuse – born 1898 in Berlin, Germany, was a philosopher who fled Germany in 1933. He worked for US intelligence during World War II and subsequently taught at several American universities. Marcuse became world famous overnight in 1964 with the publication of his book *One Dimensional Man* in which he argued that society under advanced capitalism is repressive and that man has become intellectually and spiritually complacent as a result of his psychological dependence on the consumer society. Marcuse was, however, also critical of the Soviet system. The book *One Dimensional Man* became hugely popular with students around the world.

At the age of 67

Josephine Baker – dancer and entertainer and who was Paris's most popular Music Hall artist and a star at the Folies Bergere, made a return to the Broadway stage.

Leo Tolstoy – born 1828, Yasnaya Polyana, Russian Empire. Tolstoy, regarded as one of the world's greatest novelists and the author of *War and Peace*, spent much of his life at the family estate. In his youth, he served in the army and travelled in Europe before returning home. *War and Peace* (1865-69) established him as Russia's leading novelist. Later in life, Tolstoy devoted himself to social reform and favoured a simple life. In 1898, when he was 70-years-old, he published *What is Art?*, which celebrates art's moral and religious functions and criticises fashionable art. Tolstoy rode a bicycle for the first time in his life at the age of 67.

John Dryden – born 1631 in Aldwinkle, England, was a poet, dramatist and literary critic. His plays included *Marriage A-la-Mode* and he virtually invented dramatic criticism. Dryden was named poet laureate in 1668 and in 1670 made royal historiographer. He lost royal patronage in 1688 with the accession of William III but continued to be a prolific author whose relationship with his printer/publisher was so good that a letter exists in which Dryden thanks the printer Tonson for 'two melons'. Dryden produced extensive translations of Latin poetry, including Virgil's *Aeneid*. In his late 60s, Dryden was so prolific and full of energy that he agreed to supply a publisher with 10,000 verses for £208.

Alfred Wallis – born in 1855 in Devonport, England was a seaman in the merchant service by the early 1870s. In 1876, he married. He was 20-years-old and his wife was 41, with five children. He continued to work as a deep-sea fisherman. In 1890, he started work as a dealer, buying old sails and scrap iron but in 1912 the business closed and Wallis made a living doing odd jobs, particularly for a local antiques dealer. When his wife died in 1922, Wallis who was 67, took up painting for the first time in his life. He taught himself and never had a single art lesson. His paintings are regarded as 'naïve art' in that perspective and scale are often ignored. Because he could not afford canvases or art shop quality oils, Wallis painted on bits of cardboard ripped from packing boxes and used a small number of paints bought from ships' chandlers. In 1928, a number of established artists moved to St Ives in Cornwall and Wallis found himself a member of a group of progressive artists. Despite his newfound connections and his rising fame, Wallis sold very few paintings in his lifetime and he died in poverty in a workhouse in Penzance. Sadly, he believed that his neighbours were jealous of his fame and assumed that because he was well known he must have secret wealth. He is now remembered as an important Cornish artist.

At the age of 68

Queen Victoria – born 1819, London, England. The Queen of the United Kingdom of Great Britain and Ireland and Empress of India, began to learn Hindustani at the age of 68. Her tutor (her 'official munshi') was an Indian called Abdul Karim who travelled everywhere with the Queen, even meeting monarchs and prime ministers with her. Queen Victoria learned the language well enough to keep a 13-volume diary in Hindustani. (There is no reason why older folk should not learn one or more foreign languages. Increasing age does not result in any diminution in the ability to learn a language – or anything else for that matter. The elder Cato began to learn Greek at the age of 80. And at 70, Socrates was learning to dance and play musical instruments.) There was no earthly need for Queen Victoria to learn a new language. She did it because she was never afraid to learn new things and never afraid to face a challenge.

General de Gaulle – born 1890, Lille, France. Charles Andre Joseph Marie de Gaulle was a formidable and very tall French general and politician who became President of France and remained in the position for a decade. During the First World War, de Gaulle was wounded and taken prisoner and decorated for bravery. During the German invasion of France in World War II, he was appointed Under-Secretary for War but later refused to accept his government's armistice with Nazi Germany. De Gaulle fled to Britain and led a government in exile, though he had a frosty relationship with both the British and the Americans. He became head of the provisional government of the French Republic in June 1944 but resigned in 1946 and retired in the early 1950s to write his War Memoirs. In May 1958, the Algerian War created a crisis in France and the National Assembly brought him back to power at the age of 68. De Gaulle founded the Fifth Republic and vetoed Britain's entry into the European Community. (He supported the EC only as a group of sovereign nations.) He resigned in 1969 and died the following year.

Mrs Patrick Campbell – born 1865, London, England was the actress who took the original role of Eliza Doolittle in George Bernard Shaw's play *Pygmalion* (and is remembered in literacy circles for a lengthy correspondence which she conducted with the playwright), made her first film *Riptide* in 1933 when she was 68-years-old. She must have enjoyed the experience because she later appeared in a number of other films.

Sir Charles Aubrey Smith CBE (C.Aubrey Smith) – born 1863, London England, went to South Africa to prospect for gold in 1888. He developed pneumonia and pronounced dead by the doctors looking after him. After returning to life and England, Smith became an actor. His first major role was in *The Prisoner of Zenda*. Smith also became a keen cricketer. He was a fast bowler, a useful batsman and an excellent fielder. He is regarded as one of the best bowlers ever to play. He had a curiously curved run-up which resulted in the nickname 'round the corner Smith'. He played for Sussex in the English County Championships and captained England in one Test match against South Africa. In 1933, at the age of 71, Smith made his first movie in Hollywood. These days it is relatively common for sports stars to transfer their fame to the silver screen. Eric Cantona, Vinnie Jones, Jim Brown and O.J.Smith are just four who spring to mind. But Sir C Aubrey Smith was the first sports star to make the move to the cinema. Late in his life, when he had become very famous as a film star, and, with his bushy eyebrows and handlebar moustache, one of the best known faces in the cinema, he was sitting in the pavilion at Lord's Cricket Ground when one member turned to another, nodded towards Sir C.Aubrey and said: 'Who is that fellow? He looks familiar.' 'Oh, that's Smith,' replied his companion. 'He used to play for Sussex.' In Hollywood, he founded the Hollywood Cricket Club and actors (however famous) who did not turn out to play were likely to 'incur his displeasure'. English actors who appeared in his team included David Niven, Ronald Colman, Rex Harrison, Leslie Howard, Basil Rathbone and Nigel Bruce. Films which Smith appeared in included *The Prisoner of Zenda, The Four Feathers, Rebecca, Dr Jekyll and Mr Hyde, And Then There Were*

None, *Little Women* and *Tarzan the Ape Man*. He also appeared in one of the *Thin Man* movies. All these were made when he was in his 70s and 80s.

Confucius – born 551 BC, Lu, China, was a philosopher, political theorist and teacher. He educated himself while working as a bookkeeper and managed to master the six traditional arts: ritual, music, archery, charioteering, calligraphy and arithmetic. He also studied history and poetry. He served in government posts and became Minister of Justice. He spent 12 years in self-imposed exile and then returned at the age of 68 in order to write and to teach. In the next five years, he taught over 70 disciples and wrote a series of texts called the *Five Classics*.

At the age of 69

Ronald Reagan – born 1911, Tampico, U.S. was elected President of the United States. Reagan worked as a radio sports announcer before going to Hollywood where he appeared in more than 50 movies and was twice elected President of the Screen Actors Guild. He changed his political allegiance from Democrat to Republican and was elected governor of California in 1966. Fourteen years later, at the age of 69, he defeated incumbent President Jimmy Carter, and became U.S. President. Reagan was re-elected four years later and was President until the age of 77.

Frank Lloyd Wright – born 1867, Richland Center, U.S. is widely regarded as the greatest American architect. He began his most creative and prolific years at the end of his 60s. Wright designed about 50 Prairie houses between 1900 and 1910. In the 1930s, he designed low cost houses. In 1936, at the age of 69, he built Fallingwater in Bear Run. Fallingwater is an extravagant country house, cantilevered over a waterfall. Between 1936 and 1939, he built the Johnson Wax Building which was regarded as an example of humane workplace design and subsequently, throughout his 70s, he received a huge number of major commissions.

Gilbert White – born 1720 in Selborne, England was a curate throughout his life. Regarded as one of the world's first ecologists and natural historians, White published the *Natural History and Antiquities of Selborne*, a book which was based on his letters, at the age of 69. It is said that White observations helped to shape our love of and respect for nature. Many of the letters which appear were never actually posted but were written especially for the book.

Joseph Franz Haydn – Born 1732, Rohrau, Austria, was recognised as the greatest living composer. He composed works in just about every musical genre, including 108 symphonies. He is said to have invented the string quartet and wrote 68 musical pieces for string quartets. He also wrote 48 piano sonatas and numerous other pieces of music. At the age of 69, he wrote *The Seasons*, one of the great oratorios.

At the age of 70

Francis Galton – an English explorer, eugenicist and anthropologist, invented the science of finger printing for use in police work at the age of 70. His book on the subject was called *Finger Prints* and he calculated that the chances of two individuals having the same fingerprints was around 1 in 64 billion. Galton was a cousin of Charles Darwin. In addition to his work on fingerprints, he wrote works on human intelligence, blood transfusions, criminality, twins and meteorology.

Noah Webster – born 1758, West Hartford, US. Webster, an American writer and lexicographer, published his eponymous dictionary at the age of 70. His book *The American Spelling Book*, which he published in 1783, sold over 100 million copies. He began work on the *American Dictionary of the English Language* in 1807 but did not publish the first edition until 1828. He is regarded as a vital figure in establishing the integrity of American English.

Thomas Alva Edison – born 1847, Milan, US had very little formal schooling but became an inventor. He set up a laboratory in his basement when was 10-years-old. He created the world's first industrial research laboratory in New Jersey, US. In his 70s, Edison was directing research into torpedoes and submarines. He continued to work well into his 80s (he died in 1931) and he held 1,093 patents by the time he died. He helped lay the foundation for the technological revolution and he was the first to commercialise research effectively and profitably. His research work was often financed by wealthy patrons.

Nicolaus Copernicus – born in 1473 in Frauenburg in East Prussia, mastered everything that was known about mathematics, medicine, astronomy and theology. In 1497, he was elected a canon of Frauenburg cathedral and began his astronomical studies. In 1543, at the age of 70, he published *Six Books Concerning the Revolutions of the Heavenly Orbs* which explained the motion of the planets and resolved their order. It was in this book that Copernicus argued that the Earth rotates daily around its own axis and revolves yearly around a stationary sun. Copernicus's work helped the development of a new understanding of the fundamental structure of the universe.

Barbara Woodhouse – born 1910, Rathfarnham, Ireland was a dog trainer, author and television personality. She first became famous in 1980 when her television series *Training Dogs the Woodhouse Way* turned her into an unexpected 'star' and made her a household name. She continued to appear on television, to write books and to travel around the world talking about dogs until her death in 1988.

Benjamin Disraeli – born 1804, London, England, and later known as the Earl of Beaconsfield. Disraeli was an author and politician who was twice Prime Minister. He became Prime Minister for the second time at the age of 70. He was a friend and advisor to Queen Victoria and he introduced a bill conferring on her the title Empress of India. After the Conservative party was defeated in 1880, he remained party leader and, at the age of 76, published a political novel entitled *Endymion*.

Albert Schweitzer – born 1875, Kaysersberg, Germany, was a theologian, doctor, philosopher and organist. In his youth he wrote a biography of Johann Sebastian Bach and produced an edition of Bach's organ works. He also wrote several influential books on religion. At the age of 30, he announced that he would become a mission doctor. In 1913, he and his wife moved to French Equatorial Africa (later to be renamed Gabon) and, with the aid of the local population, built a hospital and, later, a leper colony. In 1952, at the age of 77, Schweitzer was awarded the Nobel Peace Prize for his work on behalf of 'the Brotherhood of Nations'. In his 70th year, Schweitzer began working for world peace.

Enid Blyton – born 1897, London, England, the author of over 600 books for children, wrote 11 books in her 70th year. Blyton, who trained as a school teacher, is best known for her series of books, which included those involving Noddy and Big Ears, the Famous Five and the Secret Seven.

Hilda Lorna Johnstone MBE – born 1902 in York, England, participated in the Olympic Games in 1956, 1968 and 1972 at the age of 70. She took part in the equestrian dressage competition and became the oldest ever woman to take part in the Olympic Games.

Maurice Chevalier – born 1888, Paris, France, starred in the film *Gigi* and sang *Thank heavens for Little Girls*. Chevalier first appeared as a singer and comedian at the Folies-Bergere in Paris in 1909. Famous for wearing a straw hat at a jaunty angle, together with a bow tie (and the usual assortment of trousers, shirts, jackets, etc.) he went to Hollywood in 1929 and appeared in movies that helped to establish musicals as a serious and profitable film genre. Chevalier was given an honorary Academy Award during his 70th year.

Donald Trump – born 1946, New York, US, who had no political experience and who had never stood for public office before, surprised pundits, commentators and pollsters by becoming 45th President of the United States of America. Trump, a real estate developer and television personality who had inherited a property empire from his father, appalled critics and other politicians (even those within his own party) with a surprising mixture of honesty, naivety and plain speaking but won over voters with a similarly surprising mixture of honesty, naivety and plain speaking.

Benjamin Franklin – born 1706, Boston, US was an American scientist, philosopher, publisher and statesman. At the age of 12, he was apprenticed to his brother, a local printer. He taught himself to write and in 1723, moved to Philadelphia, where he founded the *Pennsylvania Gazette*. From 1730 until 1757, he wrote *Poor Richard's Almanack* which was filled with proverbs and aphorisms. As he prospered he helped found a library, a hospital, a fire department, an insurance company and a college which became the University of Pennsylvania. His inventions included bifocal spectacles and led to the development of the lightning rod. In 1776, he was a member of the committee which drafted America's

Declaration of Independence and went to France to seek help for the American Revolution. He negotiated a treaty to provide loans and military support for the United States.

W. Somerset Maugham – born 1874, in the British Embassy in Paris, France was a qualified doctor and novelist, playwright and writer of short stories. He was also a hugely influential travel writer. His simply written works show a tremendous understanding of human nature. Many of his short stories describe the confusion of Europeans in foreign surroundings. His great novels include *The Razor's Edge*, *Of Human Bondage*, *The Moon and Sixpence* and *Cakes and Ale*, and all which were turned into films. Maugham wrote *The Razor's Edge* at the age of 70, *Catalina* and *Quartet* at the age of 74, and *Encore* at the age of 78 and continued to write articles well into his late 80s. He died in 1965.

Jomo Kenyatta – born 1894, Ichaweri, British East Africa left East African highlands to become a civil servant and a political activist in Nairobi. He opposed the suggestion that Kenya, Uganda and Tanganyika be united into a single country and in 1945, he helped to organise the sixth Pan-African Confess. In 1953, he was sent to prison for seven years for directing the Mau Mau rebellion, though he denied the charges. In 1962, at the age of 70, he negotiated the terms leading to Kenya's independence and turned his country into one of the most stable and economically viable African nations.

At the age of 71

Cecil B de Mille – born 1881, Ashfield, U.S., was a film director and producer. In 1913, he joined Jesse Lasky and Samuel Goldwyn to form an early version of Paramount Communications. Their first film, *The Squaw Man* (1914) was the first full-length feature film to be produced in Hollywood. He was renowned for his extravagant sets and huge casts. He was 71 when he produced and directed *The Greatest Show on Earth* which won the Academy Award for best picture.

Coco Chanel – born 1883, Saumur, France, was really called Gabrielle Chanel. She retired at 55 but decided to un-retire at the age of 71. She celebrated by designing the Chanel suit. She opened a millinery shop in 1913 in Deauville and within five years her innovative use of fabrics and accessories was bringing her wealthy and influential customers. Her clothes, which were designed to be both simple and comfortable, revolutionised the fashion industry for decades to come. She made turtleneck sweaters popular and was the original designer of the 'little black dress' which was to become the mainstay of many wardrobes. Her shop eventually became Chanel industries, incorporating a Parisian fashion house, a textile business, perfume laboratories and a jewellery workshop. Her most successful product was 'Chanel No 5' perfume which was introduced in 1922.

Titian (originally Tiziano Vecellio) – born 1488, Venice, Italy. Taught by the Bellini family and having worked closely with Giorgione, Titian established himself as the leading painter in Venice. Many of his paintings had a religious theme but he was also interested in mythology and painted Venus many times. He is said to have reached the height of his powers with his painting *The Rape of Europa* which was one of several paintings done for Philip II of Spain and which Titian painted between the ages of 71 and 74.

Charles Darwin – born 1809, in Shropshire, England wrote *The Power of Movement of Plants* in his early 70s. Darwin studied medicine and biology and was the naturalist on board HMS Beagle during its five year scientific survey of South America and the South Seas. His discoveries during that voyage (1831-36) formed the basis of his theories of evolution. He recognised that a bird with a sharper beak might have a better chance of thriving and reproducing than birds with blunter beaks – which were less able to hunt for food. He surmised that such traits were passed on to new generations they would be predominant in future populations. This was the basis of his theory of 'natural selection', whereby advantageous variations are passed on to later generations. Darwin worked on this theory for 20 years before publishing it in his book *On the Origin of Species by Means of Natural Selection* in 1859. He continued to work until his death in 1882.

Leni Riefenstahl – born 1902 in Berlin, Germany was a dancer and an actress who became a film director and photographer. Her first film was *Das Blaue Licht* (The Blue Light). In 1933, at Adolf Hitler's suggestion, she made a propaganda film about the fifth Nuremberg Rally. As a director, she introduced a number of technical developments including slow motion, very high and low shooting angles, aerial shots, underwater filming and tracking shots. She was friends with Hitler for 12 years. When she was 60, Riefenstahl began a relationship with her assistant who was 20-years-old. They remained together until her death at the age of 101. Riefenstahl took up scuba diving in her 70s and was still diving and photographing marine life in her 90s.

Katsusuke Yanagisawa – born 1936, Japan, a retired Japanese junior high school teacher, climbed Mount Everest, becoming one of three Japanese climbers to have scaled the world's highest mountain in their 70s. His achievement was sneered at by a member of the Japan Mountaineering Association who said that Yanagisawa had been 'given a lot of support' and had 'used oxygen all the way to the top'. He climbed it though, didn't he? (The words 'green' and 'envy' spring to mind.)

Henrik Ibsen – born 1828, Skien, Norway, became theatre director and resident playwright at the National Theatre in Bergen at the rather precocious age of 23. He later travelled around Europe. He wrote *Peer Gynt*, *A Doll's House*, *Ghosts*, *An Enemy of the People*, *The Wild Duck*, *Hedda Gabler* and *The Master Builder*. He was still writing in his 70s and wrote *When We Dead Awaken* in 1899.

Colette (Sidonie-Gabrielle Colette) – born 1873, Saint-Sauveur-en-Puisaye, France, was a music hall performer and writer. Her first four Claudine novels (written in 1900-03), the reminiscences of a libertine ingenue, were published by her first husband under the pen name 'Willy'. In 1944, at the age of 71, she wrote *Gigi*, a comedy about a girl who is brought up to be a courtesan. The story was turned into a play by Anita Loos and then into a musical; it was filmed in 1958 starring Leslie Caron in the title role and also starring Maurice Chevalier and Louis Jourdan . In her early life, Colette scandalised the French public but in her later years, she became a much loved icon. She died in 1954.

At the age of 72

Karl Wallenda – born 1905, Magdeburg, Germany, was a circus acrobat. He became famous for his high wire act (known as the Great Wallendas) which included a seven person pyramid on a high wire without a safety net. His wife, Helen was balanced at the top of the pyramid. The troupe travelled in the US with the Ringling Brothers and Barnum and Bailey Circus. At the age of 72, Karl walked a tightrope between the top floors of two hotels in Miami. He died at the age of 73 when wind blew him from a wire 123 feet above a street in San Juan.

Dame May Whitty DBE – born 1865, Liverpool, England, was an English actress who, after a successful theatrical career, made her first film *Night Must Fall* in 1937 at the age of 72. She received a nomination for an Academy Award as Best Supporting Actress. She is perhaps best known for playing the vanishing lady Miss Froy in Alfred Hitchcock's film *The Lady Vanishes*, which was made in 1938 when she was 73-years-old. She received a second Academy Award nomination for her work in *Mrs Miniver*, which was made in 1942. Her last films were made in 1948 when she was 83-years-old.

Mohandas Gandhi – born 1869, Porbandar, India, (known as Mahatma Gandhi) studied law in England and took a job with an Indian firm in South Africa. He became an advocate for Indian rights and in 1906, he put into action his technique of nonviolent resistance. In 1915, he returned to India and became leader of a nationwide struggle for home rule. He organised campaigns of non-violent resistance many times – including when he was in his 60s. He also campaigned to end discrimination against India's 'untouchable class'. At the age of 72, he launched the movement that led to his country's independence in 1947. He was disappointed by the fact that the subcontinent had been divided into India and Pakistan since he had hoped for Hindu-Muslim unity. In September

1947, at the age of 78, he ended rioting in Calcutta by fasting. In January 1948, he was shot and killed by a Hindu fanatic.

Blondin – born 1824, Headin, France, (originally Jean-Francois Gravelet). Blondin was a French tightrope walker who achieved fame in 1859 by repeatedly crossing Niagara Falls on a tightrope. He went across blindfolded, in a sack, pushing a wheelbarrow, on stilts and carrying a man on his back. On one occasion, he sat down half way across and cooked an omelette. Blondin gave his last tightrope performance in 1896, at the age of 72, and died the following year.

At the age of 73

Dr Peter Mark Roget – born 1779, London, England, was a physician, inventor and philologist. In 1814, he invented a slide rule for calculating the roots and powers of numbers. He helped found the University of London in 1828. But he is best known for his *Thesaurus of English Words and Phrases*, a comprehensive collection of synonyms. He prepared the book during his retirement, beginning it at the age of 69 and finishing it at 73. He was also secretary of the Royal Society from 1827.

Konrad Adenauer – born in 1876, Cologne, Germany became Chancellor of Germany. Adenauer, who had been imprisoned by the Nazis, stressed the importance of individualism under the rule of law. He worked hard to build bridges with Gemany's former enemies – particularly France. He remained Chancellor from 1949 until 1963 when he retired. He died in 1967.

Marquis de Sade – born 1740, Paris, France, was an aristocrat, politician, revolutionary, philosopher and author best known now for his erotica. The words 'sadist' and 'sadism' are derived from his name. He believed in the freedom of the individual above all else. He spent 32 years of his life in prison where he did much of his writing. During the French Revolution, he was elected a delegate to the National Convention. In 1801, Napoleon Bonaparte ordered the arrest of the anonymous author of the books *Justine* and *Juliette*, and de Sade was duly arrested and imprisoned without trial. In the UK, his books were partly banned until 1983. At the age of 73, de Sade was still writing fiction, though some of his work was destroyed by his son (who burnt many of his father's manuscripts) and other novels were, for a variety of prurient reasons, not published until midway through the 20th century. At the age of 70, de Sade acquired a new mistress with whom he had a four year long relationship until his death in 1814.

Guiseppe Verdi – born 1813, Roncole, Italy was a composer. Verdi is particularly remembered for having created the opera as a series of integrated scenes and acts rather than as a collection of arias, duets and often only vaguely connected scenes. Verdi had retired at the age of 61, after composing his *Requiem*, but he and the poet and composer Arrigo Boito later started working together. *Otello*, written when Verdi was 73-years-old, was the first of their great operas together.

Maurice Chevalier (see above) – the French entertainer, was still working and made the film *Fanny* at the age of 73.

Colonel Harland David Sanders – born in 1890 in Indiana, United States, was still travelling 200,000 miles a year to promote the Kentucky Fried Chicken Chain. Sanders, who had adopted the title *Colonel* had sold the American part of his company Kentucky Fried Chicken but had retained control of his Canadian franchises and remained the company's symbol. Colonel Sanders opened the first restaurant in 1952 and quickly recognised the power of franchising. Within a few years, 400 franchise restaurants had been opened. Sanders, who died in 1980, became the company's spokesman, symbol and ambassador.

At the age of 74

S.J.Perelman– born 1904, New York, U.S., was an American humourist who wrote screenplays for early Marx Brothers films such as *Monkey Business* and *Horse Feathers*. His later screenplays included *Around the World in 80 Days*. He is here because, at the age of 74, he drove from Paris to Peking in an old MG motor car. The journey was a recreation of the famous 1907 Peking-to-Paris road race which had been won by Prince Borghese. The original race took months and in some places involved cars being taken apart and carried by coolies. However, instead of driving from Peking to Paris, Perelman decided to drive his 30-year-old black and red MG from Paris to Peking. It was, he said, 'the last chuck of the dice'. Perelman, who was accompanied by two male companions, attached a small trailer to the back of the car and loaded it with supplies – including 100,000 Band-Aids and 30 boxes of Lomotil. The journey started on the Champs-Elysees in Paris on September 2nd 1978, and for 27 days they drove through Central Europe, the Balkans, Turkey, Iran, Afghanistan, Pakistan and India. Unfortunately, Perelman fell out with his two fellow drivers and because there was no suitable route into China, the car had to be airlifted the last part of the journey which was, therefore, never properly completed. It was, however, a pretty brave undertaking for a 74-year-old man and a 30-year-old car who had never done anything similar before.

Franz Liszt – born 1811, Raiding, Hungary was a composer and pianist. After success in Paris in 1823, he toured Europe. Inspired by hearing the violinist Paganini, he became a serious composer and produced many classic pieces of music. He temporarily retired from playing in the late 1840s so that he could concentrate on composing. He was one of the first musicians to give solo piano recitals. He was still performing in his 70s when he toured Europe and gave a series of piano recitals.

Jean Cocteau – born 1889 Paris, France, was a poet, librettist, playwright, artist, book illustrator, designer and film director. During the First World War, he was an ambulance driver. He made the film *Le Testament d'Orphee* in 1960 when he was 71 years of age. In his final year, when he was 74, was busy decorating the church of Saint Blaise-des-Simples in Milly La Foret.

At the age of 75

Benjamin Franklin – negotiated a preliminary peace treaty with Great Britain.

Ed Delano – born 1905, USA, completed four bicycle rides across the continent of the United States. He completed his last crossing of America by bicycle in 1980 when he was 75-years-old. He took 33 days to travel the 3,100 miles so that he could attend a college reunion in Worcester, Mass. Mr Delano died at the age of 92.

Nicholas Hawksmoor – born 1661, Nottinghamshire, England was an architect who designed a number of famous churches, including six in London. He also designed a number of garden structures including the Pyramid and the Mausoleum at Castle Howard. At Blenheim Palace, he designed the Woodstock Gate. The two western towers of Westminster Abbey were designed by Hawksmoor who was still working on them when he died at the age of 75.

At the age of 76

Min Bahadur Sherchan – born 1931 in Bhurung Tatopani, West Nepal, a former British Gurkha soldier, climbed Mount Everest at the age of 76.

Auguste Rodin – born 1840, Paris, France, was a French sculptor who was repeatedly rejected by the Ecole des Beaux-Arts and for many years had to earn his living doing decorative stonework on buildings. In 1878, he was finally accepted as a sculptor when he produced a figure entitled 'The Age of Bronze', though the figure was so realistic that Rodin was accused of making a mold on a living person. He produced 'The Thinker' in 1880 and 'The Kiss' in 1886. In addition to sculpture, he produced book illustrations and many drawings, mostly of female nudes. At the age of 76, just a year before his death, he finally found the courage (and, presumably, the money for the licence) to marry Rose Beuret, the girl with whom he had lived since he was 23. It must rank as one of the longest courtships and engagements in history.

H.G.Wells – born 1866, Bromley, Kent was a novelist, historian and journalist. He studied science and, in his 30s, wrote a number of science fiction novels including *The Time Machine*, *The Invisible Man* and *The War of the Worlds*. He also agitated for a number of public causes, including the League of Nations. He abandoned science fiction and then started writing novels about lower middle class individuals – including *The History of Mr Polly* and *Kipps*. He also wrote *The Outline of History* and many other books – both fiction and non-fiction. He and his friend Jerome K Jerome (the author of comic novels such as *Three Men in a Boat*) invented miniature war games played with toy soldiers. George Orwell described Wells as 'too sane to understand the modern world'. At the age of 76, Wells successfully submitted his doctoral thesis.

Teiichi Igarishi – born 1887, Japan, a former lumberjack and forest ranger, first climbed Mount Fuji when he was 76 in memory of his wife, Ura. She died in 1975 at the age of 80. He continued to climb it every year until he was 100. Mr Igarishi started smoking at the age of 60 but stopped at the age of 96, presumably for health reasons.

At the age of 77

Clara Burton – born 1821, North Oxford, US was a nurse who founded the American Red Cross and worked during the American Civil War. At that time, there was no formal nursing training and Burton was self-taught. She campaigned for civil rights and was associated with the women's suffrage movement. In 1887, she helped in Texas during the famine. In 1888, when she was 67, she took Red Cross workers to Illinois after a tornado hit and in that same year, she took workers to Florida to help during a yellow fever epidemic. At the age of 68, she went to help out at the Johnstown Flood. And in 1897, when she was 76-years-old she sailed to Constantinople to open the first American International Red Cross headquarters in Turkey. At the age of 77, she worked in hospitals in Cuba during the Spanish-American war. She also helped victims of the Galveston hurricane in 1900. She died at the age of 90.

John Glenn – born 1921, Cambridge, US, became an astronaut and later a senator. He was the oldest of the seven astronauts selected in 1959 for the Mercury project's spaceflight training. In February 1962, he made three orbits of the earth in his space capsule called 'Friendship 7'. He retired from the space program in 1964 and served as a US senator from 1975 to 1999. In 1998, when he was 77-years-old, he made his second spaceflight and flew as a payload specialist on the Discovery mission.

At the age of 78

Marie Stopes – born 1880, Edinburgh, Scotland campaigned for eugenics and women's rights. She and her husband are remembered for founding the first birth control clinic in Britain. She edited *Birth Control News* and wrote a controversial sex manual. She was still actively promoting birth control when she was 78.

Grandma Moses, (Anna Mary Moses) – born 1860, New York, US enjoyed embroidery all her life but in her late seventies she developed arthritis which made needlework painful. Her sister suggested that she take up painting, since this would be easier for her. And so she began painting and during the next three decades (until her death at the age of 101), she produced over 1,500 paintings. To start with, she charged as little as $3 for a picture but as her fame steadily grew, so did the value of her paintings. In 1938, an art collector called Louis J.Caldor spotted her paintings in the window of a local drug store. He bought the entire stock and purchased ten more pictures from Grandma Moses herself. He paid between $3 and $5 per picture. The next year, three of Grandma Moses's paintings were included in an exhibition at New York's Museum of Modern Art.

Mae West – born 1893, New York, U.S. Ms West, an actress, playwright, screenwriter, comedian and singer was the American after whom the inflatable life vest was named. Her career in the entertainment business covered seven decades and she appeared in the film *Myra Breckinridge* at the age of 78.

Bertrand Russell (see above) – received the Nobel Prize for Literature.

Dame Edith Evans – born 1888, London, England was one of the finest actresses of the 20th century. She appeared in London and on

Broadway in plays by William Shakespeare, George Bernard Shaw and Noel Coward. She is perhaps most famous for playing Lady Bracknell in Oscar Wilde's play *The Importance of Being Earnest*. She appeared in a number of other films including *Look Back in Anger*, *Tom Jones* and *The Whisperers*. At the age of 78, she asked that her age be removed from reference books because she feared that it might prevent her getting work. It didn't.

Jean-Baptiste de Monet, Chevalier de Lamarck – born 1744, Picardy, France, was a biologist. He is credited with inventing the word 'biology'. He was an originator of the concept of the properly classified museum collection. At the age of 78, he proposed a new theory of evolution, suggesting that acquired characteristics can be transmitted to the next generation. The theory was eventually discredited.

Sir Christopher Wren – born 1632, East Knoyle, England, was an astronomer and architect. He taught astronomy at Gresham College, London and at Oxford and did not turn to architecture until he was 30-years-old, when he was hired to design the Sheldonian Theatre in Oxford. He later became King's Surveyor of Works and had a hand in rebuilding more than 50 churches which had been destroyed in the Great Fire of London. He held this post until 1718 when he was 86-years-old. He worked on St Paul's Cathedral until 1710 when he was 78-years-old. He died in 1723 and was buried in St Paul's. His resting place is commemorated with the inscription: 'Reader, if you seek a monument, look around.'

At the age of 79

Guiseppe Verdi (see above) – wrote Falstaff.

General de Gaulle (see above) – was still President of France.

Admiral Thomas Cochrane – 10th Earl of Dundonald, Marquess of Maranhao, born 1775, Hamilton, Scotland. Lord Cochrane had a tempestuous career. He was dismissed from the Royal Navy following a rather dodgy conviction for Stock Exchange fraud. He then led the rebel navies of Chile and Brazil during their wars of independence. In 1832, he was pardoned by the Crown and reinstated with the rank of Rear Admiral. His life inspired much naval fiction including C.S.Forester's Horatio Hornblower and Patrick O'Brian's Jack Aubrey. Although he was nearly 80 at the time, Cochrane volunteered for active service during the Crimean War (1853-1856). The Government considered him for a command but decided that there was a risk that Cochrane was too daring and might risk the entire fleet in a daring attack.

Dame Edith Evans (see above) – was still appearing on stage in New York – despite the fact that producers and directors were perfectly well aware of her age.

Louie Dingwall – born 1893, England, worked as a driver for the Canadian Army during World War I. Together with her husband, she built stables and a garage with a petrol pump and ran a bus service and taxi service. She trained race horses on the beach at Sandbanks in Dorset. At the age of 79, she is said to have applied for a licence to ride as a professional woman jockey. She died at the age of 89.

Sir George Cayley – born 1773, Scarborough, England. Cayley founded the science of aerodynamics and was a pioneer of aviation. By 1799, he had established the basic shape of the modern aeroplane. He built his first glider in 1804 and in 1853, he invented, designed and built a glider capable of carrying a man. In 1825, Cayley invented the caterpillar tractor and in 1839, he founded a polytechnic school in London.

At the age of 80

Grandma Moses (see above) – had her first solo art show and became established as one of America's foremost artists. Her early exhibitions also included of baked foods and preserves that had won prizes at the county fair. Over the next two decades, her paintings were exhibited throughout the United States and Europe and galleries reported that attendance records were broken. Grandma Moses' work was reproduced on greeting cards, tiles, fabrics, ceramics and her pictures were used to market a wide range of products.

Thomas Beecham – born 1879, St Helens, England was a self-taught conductor. He founded the Beecham Symphony Orchestra and co-founded the London Philharmonic Orchestra and the Royal Philharmonic Orchestra. He also founded several opera companies. He championed Mozart and his contemporaries Richard Strauss and Frederick Delius. In 1950, Beecham took the Royal Philharmonic Orchestra on an exhausting tour of the United States, Canada and South Africa. Between 1951 and 1960, Beecham conducted 92 concerts at the Royal Festival Hall. In 1958, he conducted in Argentina and in 1959 he toured the US and Canada again. Two years before his death he married his former secretary. She was 27 and he was 80.

Charles Atlas – born 1892, Acri, Italy trained himself to be the most famous bodybuilder in the world. His original name was Angelo Siciliano but he legally changed his name to Atlas when a friend told him that he looked like the statue of Atlas on top of a hotel in Coney Island. He claims that a bully really did kick sand into his face when he was a scrawny youth. At the age of 80, Atlas was still tearing telephone directories in half and this may well explain why you can never find a telephone directory when you want one.

Yuichiro Miura – born 1932, in Japan, climbed Mount Everest at the age of 80. He previously had two heart surgery operations for cardiac arrhythmia. He was also the first person to ski on Mount Everest. He descended nearly 4,200 vertical feet from the South Col in 1970.

Marc Chagall – born 1887, Vitebsk, Russia, was a painter, printmaker and designer. He studied painting in St Petersburg and moved to Paris in 1910 where he became established as an important artist. He moved to New York in 1941 where he designed sets and costumes for Stravinsky's ballet 'The Firebird'. He later produced stained-glass windows. In 1964, Chagall's ceiling for the Paris Opera was revealed. The painting required 440 pounds of paint and covers 2,600 square feet. At the age of 80, Chagall created the sets for the Metropolitan Opera's production of Mozart's 'Magic Flute'.

Leopold Stokowski – born 1882, London, England, began work in New York City in 1905 as an organist and choir director. He moved to Paris to study conducting. His conducting debut took place in 1909 when he conducted the New Symphony Orchestra at Queen's Hall in London. Later that year he became conductor of the Cincinnati Symphony Orchestra. He championed the work of many living composers (something he was to do until the end of his life) but in 1912, he resigned from his post. Two months later, he became director of the Philadelphia Orchestra. During his career, he conducted many orchestras and founded (among others) the Hollywood Bowl Symphony Orchestra. He conducted the music for a number of films. He founded the American Symphony Orchestra at the age of 80 and in the same year, he broke a leg playing football.

George Burns – a comedian famous for a wry sense of humour and for smoking cigars, acted in the film *The Sunshine Boys* (written by Neil Simon and co-starring Walter Matthau) and won an Oscar for his performance.

Bill Kane – American cowboy who was still riding in rodeos and winning.

Bob Hope – the English comedian who became an American film and theatre star, was still hosting major shows and performing for US troops overseas. Hope died at the age of 100.

Harold Soderquist – joined the American Peace Corps. He and his young wife Bertha (a mere 76-years-old) were assigned to teach in Western Samoa.

At the age of 81

Benjamin Franklin (see above) – helped to write and introduce the American constitution in his early 80s. At an age when most people are seeking a comfortable, quiet retirement, Franklin was a member of the 1787 Constitutional Convention. He helped to ensure that the Constitution was adopted in the U.S.

Victor Hugo – born 1802, Besancon, France, was a French novelist, dramatist and poet (author of *Les Miserables* and *The Hunchback of Notre-Dame*). He was the son of a general, and a well-known poet while still a teenager, and at the time of the publication of *Les Miserables* was the most successful writer in the world. In later life, he became a politician and political writer. He spent the years 1851 to 1870 in exile in the Channel Islands (both Jersey and Guernsey) because of his republican views. He published his last major works: *La Legende des siècles (Book 3)* and *L'Archipel de la Manche* at the age of 81. He had by then become a senator and a national hero of France.

Thomas Edison – an American inventor and businessman, was still inventing and acquiring patents (Edison is listed as having 1,093 patents to his name).

At the age of 82

William Gladstone – an English born politician who liked to think of himself as Welsh, became British Prime Minister for the fourth time. He was Prime Minister between 1868 and 1874, then between 1880 and 1885, in 1886 and between 1892 and 1894. While in his 80s, he introduced a bill for Home Rule for Ireland, but the bill was defeated in the House of Lords and never became law.

Winston Churchill – British Prime Minister during the Second World War, published the first part of his four-volume book entitled *A History of the English Speaking Peoples.*

Bill Kane (see above) – was still riding in rodeos.

Leo Tolstoy (see above) – wrote *I cannot be Silent*, a book attacking his Government for executing revolutionaries. Later that year, he was so fed up with all the people fussing around in his house, that he caught the first train out of town. (Sadly he contracted pneumonia, became ill on the train and died in a station master's cottage in the middle of nowhere).

Sir Roger Moore – probably most famous for his portrayal of James Bond, took part in a video protesting against the production of foie gras.

At the age of 83

Mao Tse-tung – Marxist, soldier, statesman and son of a peasant, was still Chairman of the Chinese Communist Party.

Johann Wolfgang von Goethe – born 1749, Frankfurt, Germany, was a poet, novelist, dramatist and philosopher. He finished writing *Faust*, now regarded as his masterpiece, in 1832 at the age of 83. *Faust* concerns the soul's struggle for happiness, knowledge, power and salvation. Late in his life, Goethe was regarded as a sage and visited by luminaries from all over the world. He wrote extensively on a wide range of topics including botany, optics and other scientific subjects. He died a little while after finishing writing *Faust*.

Charlie Chaplin – English born actor and director and the son of poverty stricken musical hall artists received an Oscar. Chaplin became a performer at the age of eight and while on tour in New York, he caught the eye of Mack Sennett of the Keystone Cops. At the age of 25, in his second film, developed the baggy trousers, Derby hat, oversized shoes and cane which were to be the hallmark of the 'little tramp'. He co-founded United Artists in 1919. In 1972, he was given a special Academy Award for his services to the cinema.

Dr Benjamin Spock – the author of the hugely popular and influential *Dr Spock's Baby and Child Care*, was still actively fighting for world peace. He had given up his medical practice at the age of 64 and devoted himself to fighting the Vietnam War and promoting a vegan diet for children. He was arrested many times for civil disobedience. He was on one occasion arrested for praying on the White House lawn.

Sir Barnes Wallis – inventor of the bouncing bomb used by Guy Gibson's Dambusters during World War II. The bombs were used to destroy the Mohne and Eder dams in Germany's industrial Ruhr valley and had a significant impact on the outcome of the war – not least in that they gave great encouragement to the British people. The charismatic Gibson helped bring America into the Second World War. When still in his 80s, Wallis was chief of Aeronautical Research and Development for British Aircraft Corporation.

At the age of 84

Marian Hart – (who had learned to fly at 54) completed another solo transatlantic flight in a small, single engine aircraft. She made seven solo flights across the Atlantic. She lived until she was 98.

Dr Benjamin Spock (see above) – paediatrician and bestselling author, won 3rd place in a rowing contest, crossing four miles of the Sir Francis Drake Channel between Tortola and Normal Island in two and a half hours. He credited his good health and strength to his love of life and his lifestyle. Spock lived on a boat for much of his later life and only moved into a house at the age of 95 when advised to do so by his physician.

George Burns (see above) – the comedian, had a hit record in 1980. His recording of *I Wish I Was 18 Again* hit number 49 in the Billboard Top 50. This was his first recording success since 1933 when he and Gracie Allen had a hit comedy record.

Henri Matisse – the prolific painter, sculptor and graphic artist, was still painting. He designed the Chapelle du Rosaire at Vence as a gift for the Dominican nuns who were caring for him.

Guiseppe Verdi (see above) – wrote Stabat Mater.

Claude Monet – was still painting.

Somerset Maugham – was still writing.

At the age of 85

Carl Jung – finished work on *Man and his Symbols*, his best-known work.

Mae West (see above) – made the film *Sextette*.

Theodore Mommsen – received a Nobel Prize.

Marcus Porcius Cato – the Roman statesman, author and orator was still campaigning to destroy Carthage before it became a threat to the Roman Empire.

At the age of 86

Louise Weiss – French author, journalist and feminist, was elected an MEP, representing a French region. She had been a suffragette in Paris in 1935. In 1979, at the age of 86, she was elected a French member of the European Parliament, having stood as a candidate of the Gaullist Party. (The Gaullist Party was named after General Charles de Gaulle who dominated France in the years after the Second World War.) Louise Weiss remained an MEP until her death at the age of 90. The main parliament building in Strasbourg is named after her.

Francis Peyton Rous – an American who was born in 1879, received the Nobel Prize for discovering the role of viruses in the transmission of some types of cancer. In 1911, Rous observed that a malignant tumour growing on a domestic chicken could be transferred to another bird through a virus. He was nominated for a Nobel Prize in 1926 but finally received one 40 years later. Curiously, his daughter, Marni, married another Nobel Prize winner, Alan Lloyd Hodgkin.

Elizabeth Blackwell – an English born physician and the first woman doctor, was still working in medical practice. Her family moved to the United States in 1832, when she was 11-years-old. She studied medicine by reading books and hiring instructors. Medical schools rejected her applications until, in 1847, at the age of 26, she was accepted by the Geneva Medical College (later renamed Hobart College). She was ostracised but graduated at the top of her class. In 1857, she founded the New York Infirmary, staffed entirely by women and subsequently introduced a course of medical education for women.

Jean-Auguste-Dominique Ingres – born 1780, Montauban France, was still painting and producing great works of art until the year of his death. Ingres had become France's most popular society portraitist. His most notable later works are female nudes and his influence is seen in the work of Edgar Degas, Pierre-Auguste Renoir and Pablo Picasso. In 1862, at the age of 82, Ingres painted *The Turkish Bath*, rendered in the circular format of the earlier masters whom he had always admired. The painting showed a number of voluptuous female nudes. In 1864, at the age of 84, he painted another masterpiece, entitled *Oedipus and the Sphinx*.

Coco Chanel (see above) – was still deciding what women around the world should wear.

Dame Agatha Christie – born 1980, Torquay, England was still writing novels. *The Guinness Book of Records* lists Christie as the best-selling novelist of all time. Her books have sold around two billion copies, putting her behind only the Bible and Shakespeare in total sales. Her most famous characters are Hercule Poirot and Miss Marple. She is the world's most translated author and her books have been translated into 103 languages. Her most successful novel, *And Then There Were None* has sold over 100 million copies. (The book was first published under the title *Ten Little Niggers*.) Her play *The Mousetrap*, opened at the Ambassadors Theatre in London in 1952 and was still running in 2017 after 25,000 performances.

At the age of 87

Albert Schweitzer (see above) – helped build half a mile of road near to his hospital, and then also designed and helped to build a stone bridge.

Frank Lloyd Wright – proposed building a skyscraper one mile high.

Mary Baker Eddy – founded the *Christian Science Monitor*. In 1866, at the age of 45 she had a severe fall and healed herself by reading the *New Testament*. She then founded Christian Science and spent some years evolving her system. In 1875, at the age of 54, she published *Science and Health with Key to the Scriptures*. In 1879, she founded 'The Church of Christ, Scientist'.

George Burns (see above) – comedian was still performing and telling jokes which he admitted were older than he was.

Konrad Adenauer (see above) – was still Chancellor of Germany, though he retired at this age.

At the age of 88

Michelangelo (see above) – worked on the Rondanini Pieta.

Konrad Adenauer (see above) – decided it was time to start work on his memoirs.

Pablos Casals – born 1876, Vendrell, Spain, was a cellist and conductor. Casals refused to return to Spain after Franco took power and, based in Puerto Rico, he toured the world both as a soloist and as a conductor. Casals was still giving touring and concerts at the age of 88 at a time when most people are being encouraged to spend their remaining years sitting in a plastic armchair in an old folks' home.

Bertrand Russell (aka 3rd Earl Russell) – born 1872, Trellech, Wales, was a British logician and philosopher worked tirelessly for pacifism and nuclear disarmament. To academics, he is known both for his work in mathematical logic and for his philosophy. More widely, he is remembered for his campaigning on behalf of a number of social and political causes, particularly pacifism and nuclear disarmament. He was born into the British nobility. His pacifism during the First World War resulted in him losing his lectureship at Cambridge and being imprisoned. His books included *A History of Western Philosophy* which was a best-seller. At the age of 88, he resigned from the Campaign for Nuclear Disarmament to form the far more militant Committee of 100.

Grandma Moses – was named 'Young Woman of the Year' by *Mademoiselle* magazine. A documentary was made and she wrote her autobiography.

At the age of 89

Dr Albert Schweitzer (see above) – was still running his hospital in West Africa.

Artur Rubenstein – born 1887, Lodz, Poland was a pianist. Between 1932 and 1937, he stopped performing in public in order to improve his technique. Afterwards, he moved to the US and was regarded as a 'giant of 20th century music'. He was active throughout his 80s and was still giving concerts at the age of 89. At that age, he gave a recital at the Carnegie Hall in New York although his eyes were so bad that he could not see the piano keys, let alone read any music. However, critics agreed that he had played better than ever.

Michelangelo – born 1475, Caprese, Italy, was a sculptor, painter, poet and architect. He worked as a sculptor for Lorenzo de Medici and then moved to Rome where he was commissioned to produce the Pieta (now in St Peter's Basilica). His 'David' was commissioned for the cathedral of Florence. He painted the ceiling of the Sistine Chapel between 1508 and 1512. He devoted the last 30 years of his life to working on the 'Last Judgement' fresco in the Sistine Chapel and was working on St Peter's Basilica in Rome at his death in 1564.

Bertrand Russell (see above) – was imprisoned for a second time for inciting civil disobedience.

At the age of 90

Grandma Moses (see above) – was still painting in 1950 at the age of 90, and her paintings were attracting prices of $10,000 or more.

Colonel Saunders (see above) – was still promoting Kentucky Fried Chicken. By this time, there were 6,000 outlets in 48 countries.

Duncan MacLean – born 1884, Gourock, Scotland, was an athlete and coach who began his life appearing in music halls as a singer and general entertainer. He appeared on stage as 'Dan O'Scott', dressed in an all-white outfit, including a kilt. He wrote many of the songs he sang. In 1931, he helped to form the Veterans' Athletic Club. At the age of 90, he ran 200 metres in 44 seconds. A year later, he ran 100 metres in 21.27 seconds.

Bertrand Russell (see above) – was still active in global politics.

Leopold Stokowski (see above) – now hopefully recovered from his broken leg, recorded 20 albums during his 90th year and conducted the London Symphony Orchestra in a concert which he had first conducted 60 years earlier.

P.G.Wodehouse – born 1881, Guildford, England, was a novelist, short story writer, lyricist and playwright. He lived much of his adult life in France and the U.S. He is best known as the creator of Bertie Wooster and his valet Jeeves. Wodehouse is credited with having created an entirely fictional world of his own. Wodehouse wrote more than 90 books and 20 film scripts and collaborated with musicians such as Jerome Kern in writing musical comedies. Wodehouse wrote the last Jeeves and Wooster book at the age of 90 but carried on writing other novels.

Marc Chagall – at the age of 90, Chagall became the first living artist to be exhibited at the Louvre museum. He died in 1985.

Pablo Picasso – born 1881, Malaga Spain, was a sculptor, printmaker, stage designer and ceramicist. He moved to Paris in 1904. His so-called 'blue period' lasted from 1901 to 1904 and was followed by his 'rose period'. Between 1909 and 1912, he worked closely with George Braque with whom he developed what was later known as 'cubism'. The Spanish Civil War inspired his best-known work, the vast 'Guernica', which was completed in 1937. He was still drawing and engraving at the age of 90.

Albert Schweitzer (see above) – was still caring for patients at his hospital in Gabon.

Eamon de Valera – born 1882, New York, US, was President of the Republic of Ireland. De Valera's political career lasted from 1917 to 1973 and he served several terms as head of government and head of state. De Valera was made President of the Republic of Ireland in 1959 and was re-elected in 1966 when he was 84-years-old. He retired in 1973 when he was 90-years-old. He was then the oldest head of state in the world.

Baron Alexander von Humboldt – born 1769, Berlin, Germany was a naturalist and explorer. In 1792, he established a technical school for miners and from 1799 onwards, he explored Central and South America. He discovered the connection between the Amazon and Orinoco rivers and surmised that altitude sickness was caused by a lack of oxygen. His work helped found the science of climatology and he studied the relationships between a region's geography and its flora and fauna. At the age of 65, he began writing Kosmos, an account of the structure of the universe as it was then known, and he finished this just before he reached the age of 90.

At the age of 91

Thomas Hobbes – born 1588, Westport, England, Hobbes was an English philosopher and political theorist. Hobbes travelled in Europe (where he talked with Galileo) but in England, his support for absolutism resulted in him being endangered by rising antiroyalist sentiment. Hobbes fled to Paris in 1640 where he taught the future King Charles II of England. In Paris, he wrote *Leviathan* in 1651. The thesis of the book was that the sovereign should have absolute power on the basis of a social contract in which individuals protect themselves by obeying the sovereign in all matters. Hobbes returned to England in 1651. In 1666, when Hobbes was 78-years-old, Parliament threatened to investigate him as an atheist. Charles II protected Hobbes and gave him a pension of £100 a year. The result of Parliament's intervention was that Hobbes could no longer publish anything in England and his work was subsequently printed in Amsterdam. In 1672, at the age of 84, Hobbes published an autobiography in Latin verse and in 1675, at the age of 87, he published complete translations of both *Iliad* and *Odyssey*. He was still writing books at the age of 91.

Frank Lloyd Wright (see above) – was almost 92-years-old when his Guggenheim Museum in New York was completed. The Guggenheim has no separate floor levels but uses a spiral ramp instead of staircases. Wright is often considered America's greatest architect. He is remembered most for popularising the idea that buildings should be in harmony with their environment and with the people who will use them.

Adolph Zukor – born 1873, Ricse, Austria-Hungary, was an American filmmaker and the founder of Paramount Pictures. In the late 1920s, Zukor was producing 60 feature films a year. He pioneered the concept of the distributor charging the exhibitor a percentage of the box office receipts. He was still chairman of Paramount Pictures when he died at the age of 103.

At the age of 92

Michel Eugene Chevreul – published work on the theories of matter.

At the age of 93

Antonio Stradivari – born 1644, Cremona, Milan was a maker of musical instruments. He established his own business in his home town and made many instruments including harps, lutes, mandolins and guitars. However, after 1680, he concentrated on making violins. In 1690, he invented the 'long strad'. He devised the modern form of the violin bridge and his proportions for the violin are still used. Violinists believe that the shallower body as devised by Stradivari gives a more powerful tone than was previously available. Stradivari was at his peak between 1700 and 1720 and was still making violins at the age of 93, shortly before his death.

P.G.Wodehouse (see above) – the creator of Bertie Wooster and Jeeves the butler, was still writing novels.

At the age of 94

George Bernard Shaw (see above) – wrote his play *Why She Would Not* in seven days, just before his 94th birthday – he died at the age of 94 of injuries which he sustained after falling out of a tree in his garden which he was pruning.

George Burns (see above) – the comedian, was still performing at the age of 94. He performed in *Schenectady*, New York, 63 years after his first performance there. He died at the age of 100.

Bertrand Russell (see above) – was still campaigning for peace and he was in his 94th year when he set up the International War Crimes Tribunal in Stockholm.

At the age of 95

Nola Ochs – born 1911, Kansas, US, received a college degree from Fort Hays State University, Kansas at the age of 95. She was certified by Guinness World Records as the world's oldest college graduate.

Eli Wallach – born 1915 New York, US had a career which spanned six decades. He made over 90 films and was one of the greatest character actors of all time. His movies included *The Magnificent Seven, The Good, the Bad and the Ugly, The Two Jakes* and *The Godfather Part III*. At the age of 95, he acted in *Wall Street: Money Never Sleeps* and *The Ghost Writer*.

At the age of 96

Harry Bernstein – born 1910, Stockport, England spent his life reading scripts and acting as a magazine editor. He had his first book published at the age of 96. The book was entitled *The Invisible Wall: A Love Story that Broke Barriers.* He started writing to help him cope with loneliness after the death of his wife Ruby, to whom he had been married for 67 years. His second book, published in 2008, when he was 97, was entitled *The Dream.* His third book was published in 2009 and entitled *The Golden Willow.* Bernstein died at the age of 101.

At the age of 97

Martin Miller – born 1892, Indiana, US, was still working fulltime as a lobbyist in his 90s. He was campaigning for more rights and better benefits for older people at the age of 97. He testified at hearings and meetings of the legislature and at various boards and commissions, throughout the year – representing the interests of senior citizens. He volunteered to become his home state's No 1 advocate for the elderly in 1957 and rarely failed to attend the Indiana General Assembly.

At the age of 98

Fred Streeter – born 1879, Pulborough, England, was Britain's best-known gardener. He worked in a number of gardens, becoming a head gardener while still in his 20s. In 1901, he met his wife, Hilda. The couple were married until her death in 1966. Streeter, who worked on both radio and television, was still broadcasting on the BBC radio at the age of 98, with his final broadcast transmitted on the day he died. He never used a script.

At the age of 99

Beatrice Wood – born 1893, San Francisco, US, was an artist and potter, actress and sculptor. She was known as the 'Mama of Dada' because of her involvement in the Avant Garde movement. She also became a leading ceramicist. At the age of 90, Wood became a writer (after encouragement from anais Nin). When asked for the secret of her longevity she said: 'I owe it all to chocolate and young men.' She was still working and exhibiting her latest work at the age of 99. She lived to be 105.

At the age of 100

Teiichi Igarishi (see above) – climbed Mount Fuji again, though he did carry a cane. He wore thick socks but no shoes.

Grandma Moses (see above) – celebrated her 100th birthday, and New York Governor Nelson Rockefeller announced that it was 'Grandma Moses Day'. She was featured on the cover of *LIFE* magazine. A book for children entitled *Grandma Moses Story Book* was published.

Michel Eugene Chevreul (see above) – gave the first photo interview.

Melquiades Ortiz – born 1861, Mexico was still actively farming, using a horse and a walking plough well after his 100th birthday. He was still farming and delivering the mail until shortly before he died at the age of 109.

Fauja Singh – born 1911, Punjab, India, broke a number of world records in one day in Canada. He ran the 100 metres in 23.14 seconds, 200 metres in 52.23 seconds, the 400 metres in 2 minutes 13.48 seconds, the 800 metres in 5 minutes 32 seconds, the 1500 metres in 11 minutes 27.81 seconds, the mile in 11 minutes 53.45 seconds, the 3000 metres in 24 minutes 52.47 seconds and the 5000 metres in 49 minutes 57.39 seconds. Five of these were world records for his age group. Three days later Singh, a vegetarian, became the first 100-year-old to finish a marathon. He took eight hours 11.06 minutes to complete the course. He completed another marathon (in Hong Kong) five weeks away from his 102nd birthday. He then announced his intention to retire from competitive running but said that he would continue running for pleasure, health and charity.

And, finally, I must mention Charles Smith who was, in 1842, in Liberia and who was taken to the US as a slave and sold in New Orleans to a man called Smith (hence his name). Mr Smith was forced to retire from a citrus farm in 1955, at the age of 113, because he was officially considered too old to climb trees. I applaud the official who apparently considered 112 to be an acceptable age for climbing trees.

The fact is that most centenarians keep working for as long as they are able (or have, at least, kept themselves busy).

The one thing they have in common is that they never accept the nonsense that just because you are old in years you must allow yourself to be stuffed in a corner until you die.

Note from Vernon Coleman:
If you have found this book inspirational, I would be enormously grateful if you would write a short, and hopefully positive, review.

For details of more books by Vernon Coleman please see his Amazon biography, type in 'Vernon Coleman kindle books' on Amazon or visit www.vernoncoleman.com

Made in the USA
Monee, IL
25 March 2021